Silent Master

Mathias Simiyu

Published by Mathias Simiyu, 2025.

SILENT MASTER

First edition. September 30, 2025.

ISBN: 979-8232291518

Written by Mathias Simiyu.

Also by Mathias Simiyu

Money
Football
Break the Chain
Stay Awake
Men Resist Death
New World
Silent Master
Before You Call Her Wife
The Environment Shape You

Table of Contents

To every human voice fading in the noise of machines—may you never forget your silent strength.

The loudest revolutions are silent—the kind where machines replace men.

Introduction — The New Servitude They told us machines would free us. They promised time, ease, progress.

But instead, we woke into a world where the first thing we touch in the morning and the last thing we touch at night is not another human being, not even our own breath — but a small glowing screen that dictates the rhythm of our existence.

We thought we had built servants.

But slowly, the servants became masters.

Not doing was never an escape; it was an accumulation. Every act we surrendered to machines

— every calculation, every reminder, every judgment outsourced — stacked upon the other until the weight bent us. At first, we thought we had escaped work. In truth, we had multiplied it, only moving it outside ourselves. The price of convenience was not freedom. It was servitude in disguise.

Machines have intelligence, yes. But intelligence is not wisdom. Intelligence stores; wisdom chooses. Intelligence collects; wisdom resists. Intelligence calculates; wisdom judges.

Machines can collect our memories, count faster than we ever will, and replay information without error. But they do not ask why. They do not know when to stop. They do not suffer for us.

The tragedy is this: humanity has both intelligence and wisdom. Yet we have allowed ourselves to be driven not by wisdom, but by feelings of comfort, fear, and dependence. We trade judgment for convenience, reflection for automation, and freedom for efficiency.

Look at the workplace. An employee who does not know how to operate a machine is useless. Break a machine, and you are fired. The measure of human worth is no longer effort, creativity, or resilience, but obedience to machines. In the modern economy, jobs are less about serving humanity's purpose and more about maintaining machinery — physical or digital.

Look at health. The hospital was built as a sanctuary of healing, yet it has become a cathedral of machinery. The hum of monitors, the blinking of lights, the charts and readouts often overshadow the human touch. A machine's reading can seal a fate, and sometimes, the shock of its cold certainty kills faster than the illness itself. Death has become mechanical. We call it care, but sometimes, it is surrender.

Look at life itself. The first breath of the morning is interrupted by a phone; the last thought of the night is closed by its glow. We cannot imagine communication without it, work without it, survival without it. Phones command our attention more faithfully than lovers, more strictly than teachers, more endlessly than rulers. They are the first altar of our devotion.

We have become slaves of machines — and what makes it worse is that most of us call this slavery "help."

But unless the unconscious is made conscious, it will continue to direct your life, and you will call it fate. Machines are not evil; our surrender is. Artificial intelligence is not wisdom; it is stored thought. A phone is not a god; it is a tool. But when tools rise above their masters, when we obey the helper instead of mastering it, we no longer live as humans — we live as extensions of what we created.

This book is not a rejection of machines. It is a call to reclaim control. Machines were made to make life easier, not to replace humanity. They should serve, not enslave. They should amplify, not dictate.

If we are to remain human in a world of growing machinery, we must see the chains, name them, and break them where they bind us most invisibly.

Chapter One: The Birth of Slavery Every chain begins as a thread.

No one wakes up enslaved overnight.

The birth of machine slavery was subtle, almost invisible. It began not with the command of force, but with the whisper of help. We invited machines into our lives because they solved problems. A wheel moved faster than our legs, a plough tilled deeper than our hands, a calculator counted quicker than our brains. And so, with every invention, humanity stepped into greater power.

But power is a double edge. The moment you stop questioning it, it turns against you.

The early machines were tools — extensions of muscle, amplifiers of strength. But slowly, as machines learned not just to move but to decide, the relationship shifted. Machines no longer only obeyed; they guided. They told us the shortest road, the fastest route, the most efficient method. And in listening, we forgot to question. We obeyed because it was easier than thinking. Slavery begins with obedience without reflection.

Consider the first clock. Time was once measured by the sun, the moon, the rhythm of life itself. When clocks arrived, they disciplined us. They told us when to wake, when to work, when to rest. They organized societies with precision — but they also enslaved humanity to artificial rhythm. A farmer once knew his body, his soil, his sky. Now he knew only the tick of a clock.

Consider the typewriter, and later, the computer. They multiplied speed, accuracy, productivity. But they also changed what we value: not depth, but output. Not truth, but efficiency. Not patience, but speed. Work became chained not to wisdom but to machinery.

Consider the industrial machine. Factories produced goods on scales unimaginable, but the human became part of the assembly line — no longer creator, but cog. The worker was judged by how well he served the machine, not how well the machine served him.

Each of these threads seemed harmless. A clock is useful. A computer is powerful. A factory feeds millions. But step by step, the thread wound tighter. Humanity, instead of mastering its tools, began adjusting itself to fit the demands of its tools.

Slavery was born not when machines appeared, but when we stopped asking: "Who serves whom?"

The tragedy of modernity is not invention. It is the silent handover of authority. We believed machines were neutral, but in truth, every machine carries an ethic: what it measures, what it ignores, what it demands. When we align ourselves to these ethics without resistance, we surrender sovereignty.

This is why the first victims of machine slavery were not the poor but the ordinary. The farmer who woke to the clock. The worker who obeyed the factory. The student who studied to fit a machine-graded test. The patient who trusted a readout more than their own body.

We think slavery must look like chains and whips. But slavery is simply this: the replacement of choice with obedience.

The birth of machine slavery is the story of a slow surrender. And unless we recognize its origins, we cannot imagine its end.

Chapter Two: The Algorithm Throne

The new kings of the world do not wear crowns.

They do not live in palaces, nor do they raise armies of men.

Their power is quieter, cleaner, more invisible — but infinitely stronger. They are algorithms.

An algorithm is, in its essence, a set of instructions. Simple, almost childish in its logic: if this, then that. Yet layered, multiplied, and fed with oceans of human behavior, algorithms have become thrones of hidden power.

Today, they decide what you see, what you ignore, who you talk to, what you desire, and how you vote. They sculpt your perception of reality without your permission. You think you are choosing, but the path has been lit before you took your first step.

The throne of the algorithm is built on three pillars:

1. Attention as Currency

Once, gold was wealth. Then oil. Now it is your focus. Every second you look at a screen, every pause, every click, every scroll is captured, measured, and sold.

> Social media does not exist to connect you; it exists to harvest you. You are not the customer.

You are the product.

1. Prediction as Power

The algorithm does not just record your behavior; it predicts it. It knows you will pause at an image, laugh at a joke, rage at a headline.

This prediction becomes manipulation. You think you are free because you can choose, but in truth, the range of your choices has been narrowed by invisible hands.

1. Obedience through Seduction

Unlike the whips of old, algorithms enslave by delight. They give you what you like, what you fear, what you crave. They whisper to your emotions until you believe the whisper is your own thought.

The slave who loves his chains never breaks them.

The throne is invisible, but its commands are real. People stay awake not because they choose to, but because the feed never ends. People buy not because they need, but because a targeted ad knows their weakness better than they do. People argue, rage, divide, and destroy relationships not because they hate each other, but because algorithms profit from conflict more than harmony.

This is the new slavery: to live inside realities crafted by machines that feed on your very being. And the tragedy? We call this freedom. We say, "I can see whatever I want, whenever I want." But in truth, you see only what the algorithm allows.

The throne stands because we kneel without knowing. Chapter Three: Chains of Convenience

Slavery does not always feel like chains. Sometimes, it feels like comfort.

The most dangerous prisons are the ones that feel like luxury. Convenience has become the sweetest drug of modern life — and the most suffocating.

Machines promised to make life easier, and they have. But in making life easier, they made us weaker. We have traded resilience for reliance, skill for simplicity, and memory for automation. Look at maps. Once, travelers memorized roads, stars, landmarks. Now, GPS directs every turn. Miss one instruction, and you are lost — not because the road disappeared, but because the skill to read it is gone.

Look at communication. Once, letters carried meaning, patience, and presence. Now, instant messages reduce love to emojis and thought to abbreviations. We are constantly connected yet deeply disconnected.

Look at work. Once, craftsmanship was pride; the worker's touch mattered. Now, automation replaces effort. A button does what a man once did with his whole body. Skills vanish into the silence of machinery.

Convenience feels like progress, but its chains are heavy:

1. Dependence

The more machines do, the less we remember, the less we try. Eventually, we cannot function without them.

1. Impatience

We no longer wait. We no longer endure. The machine's speed has set a standard that human life cannot match. Waiting becomes unbearable, slowness intolerable.

1. Fragility

A power outage, a broken system, a malfunction — and entire lives collapse. A simple failure of convenience becomes a catastrophe because we no longer hold the skills to survive without it.

Ancient people lived longer not only in years but in resilience. They knew how to walk without maps, heal without machines, live without constant assistance. Death was optional because life was strong. Today, life is fragile because it is outsourced.

Convenience has enslaved us with velvet ropes. We think we are kings because everything bends to our command, but in truth, we are children who cannot live without toys.

To break these chains, we must remember this: machines were made to assist, not to replace. A helper is not a master. A tool is not a god.

The test of freedom is simple: if the machine fails, can you still live?

Chapter Four: The Digital Pharaohs Every age has its empires.

Once, kings and emperors ruled with armies, pyramids, and swords.

Today, the rulers are unseen — they sit behind glowing screens, lines of code, and vast digital networks.

We call them Big Tech, but they are the Digital Pharaohs.

Like the pharaohs of old, they command armies — not of men with spears, but of machines, satellites, and algorithms. Like the pharaohs of old, they build monuments — not pyramids of stone, but digital pyramids of data that stretch higher than any monument before them.

And like the pharaohs of old, they require labor.

But this time, we are not paid workers. We are the labor itself.

Every click, every photo uploaded, every word typed, every second scrolled — all of it builds their empire. We are brickmakers of the digital age, building temples of data that we will never own.

These pharaohs rule in silence. They own our attention.

They dictate our communication. They map our movements.

They decide what is acceptable thought and what is not.

And worse: they do it while making us believe it is all for our benefit.

Just as ancient slaves built pyramids thinking it was for the gods, we build these data monuments thinking it is for connection, convenience, and entertainment. But the gods of today are profit and power — and we are the sacrifice.

The Digital Pharaohs have three weapons:

1. Surveillance

Every action is tracked, every location logged, every preference stored. Privacy is no longer a right but a luxury, and most have sold it for free apps and entertainment.

1. Control of Speech

What cannot be said online may as well not exist. Thought itself is filtered, not by open censorship, but by silent invisibility. The algorithm buries what it dislikes. You are silenced, not with chains, but with obscurity.

1. Economic Dependence

Jobs, businesses, livelihoods all run through digital systems. To be cut off from these systems is to be exiled from modern life.

The pharaohs of the past ruled by fear of the whip. The Digital Pharaohs rule by fear of disconnection. To be offline is to be invisible, and to be invisible is to be powerless.

But here lies the truth: a pharaoh is only powerful because the people obey. A digital empire only survives because we feed it. If humanity chose to step away, the empire would collapse overnight.

The question is not whether the Pharaohs are strong. The question is: how long will humanity bow before realizing the gods are man-made?

Chapter Five: The Illusion of Ownership

Ownership once meant control. To own a thing was to command it, use it, shape it, and claim responsibility for it. But in the age of machines, ownership has become an illusion.

You think you own your phone. But does it not own your time?

You think you own your car. But without GPS, would you know where to go? You think you own your job. But if the system fails, are you still valuable?

Ownership is no longer about possession. It is about who controls whom. The illusion of ownership comes in many forms:

1. The Phone as Master

We say, "I use my phone." But how much of your day does it command? Who do you answer faster: a loved one, or a notification? Who interrupts your sleep, your meals, your silence? The phone is not a tool anymore; it is a leash.

1. The Car as Director

Cars once gave freedom — to travel, to explore, to discover. Now, without machines to direct them, most are lost. The GPS speaks, and we obey. The car is no longer your servant; it is your guide.

1. The Job as Algorithm

   In the modern economy, your worth is measured not by human judgment, but by metrics.

Numbers, charts, and performance software decide who stays and who leaves. Your boss is no longer a person; it is a machine.

1. The Cloud as Cage

We place our memories, our photos, our thoughts into digital storage. But do we really own them? A company can lock an account, delete a file, erase a life's worth of history with one command. Our most personal possessions no longer live in our homes but in servers we will never see.

This illusion is the cruelest chain, because it makes us believe we are in control. A man in chains knows he is enslaved. But a man who mistakes his leash for freedom will never break it. True ownership is not having a machine in your hand. It is being able to live without it. If the machine fails and you collapse, then you did not own the machine — it owned you.

Ownership must be redefined:

To own a tool is to master it, not to depend on it.

To own your life is to remain whole without machines.

To own freedom is to resist the illusion that convenience is control.

We have mistaken possession for power. But possession without mastery is slavery.

Chapter Six – Breaking the Chains

Slavery ends not when the master releases you, but when you refuse to kneel. Machines will never stop demanding our attention, our obedience, our trust. They will grow faster, smarter, more convincing. They will whisper louder into the ears of a distracted generation. But machines cannot enslave the man who remembers he was never born to bow.

To break the chains is not to destroy machines. It is to reclaim your place above them. To remind yourself that they are tools, not gods. Servants, not rulers. Helpers, not authorities. The true rebellion begins in the smallest acts:

To wake up and not touch your phone first.

To listen to your soul before you listen to the machine. To ask questions that no search engine can answer. To live with wisdom, not just intelligence.

To work with machines, but never for them.

The future is not written in code. It is written in choice. And choice belongs only to the human heart.

History will not remember this age for its technology. It will remember it for its surrender. It will ask: how did humanity, the wisest of creatures, choose to kneel before its own creation?

But history will also remember the few who refused. The few who stood awake while the crowd slept. The few who said: "Machines are not my masters. I am."

You, reader, are one of those few. Otherwise, you would not hold this book in your hands. The machines will keep advancing. The world will keep worshipping them. But the power remains yours—always yours. To live with wisdom. To think beyond data. To feel beyond signals. To choose beyond programming.

Do not fear the machine. Fear the forgetting of yourself.

For when man remembers who he is, no machine—no matter how powerful—can enslave him. We are not here to obey the helper, but to master it

It's not too late to turn around because the one who enslaves us has no idea yet.

Don't miss out!

Visit the website below and you can sign up to receive emails whenever Mathias Simiyu publishes a new book. There's no charge and no obligation.

https://books2read.com/r/B-A-XMYME-HOSXG

Did you love *Silent Master*? Then you should read *Stay Awake*[1] by Mathias Simiyu!

[2]

View the world as it's without a mask , try to remove the one you hold and confuse you are .

1. https://books2read.com/u/4XOr2e
2. https://books2read.com/u/4XOr2e

Also by Mathias Simiyu

Money
Football
Break the Chain
Stay Awake
Men Resist Death
New World
Silent Master
Before You Call Her Wife
The Environment Shape You

About the Author

A creative thinker , a philosopher who chose to see the world as it's without a mask chose to be dislike stayed a life of betrayal dislike and mistreat

From Kenya Bungoma chose to share his view about the world as it's

www.ingramcontent.com/pod-product-compliance
Lightning Source LLC
LaVergne TN
LVHW101618210926
848480LV00009B/825